Large Print Joke Book

100 Jokes and Fun Activities for the More Mature Population (That's Just Fancy Terms for Old)

Kiosk 2000 Publisher

Thank you for your purchase.

Please consider leaving a review!

Bonus Newslettres

Free PDF

Memory Journal

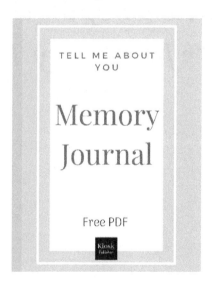

www.kiosk-2000.com

purposes only. All effort has been executed to present accurate, up to date, reliable, complete information. No warranties of any kind are declared or implied. Readers acknowledge that the author is not engaged in the rendering of legal, financial, medical or professional advice. The content within this book has been derived from various sources. Please consult a licensed professional before attempting any techniques outlined in this book.

By reading this document, the reader agrees that under no circumstances is the author responsible for any losses, direct or indirect, that are incurred as a result of the use of the information contained within this document, including, but not limited to, errors, omissions, or inaccuracies.

Table of Contents

Introduction

As soap is to the body, so laughter is to the soul - Jewish Proverb

(If you use soap regularly that is!)

While laughing out loud hysterically is a sure way to get the people around you to leave you the heck alone, there's an even greater benefit to humor and laughter that many people don't even know about.

You see, our brains release a chemical called dopamine that's a sort of "feel-good" hormone, and it helps us feel happy and jolly. Dopamine is involved in a pathway in our brains that's responsible for motivation, learning, and even emotions. Stimulating this area of the brain by laughing has shown to improve long term memory as well as enhance problem-solving abilities (Henderson, 2015). That means a laugh a day could probably make you smarter, remember better, and even make you feel happier.

I'm about to go into some scientific mumbo jumbo, so bear with me. Old people know better than most that as time goes on, memory becomes somewhat distorted. You might forget why you walked into the kitchen or forget to brush your dentures at night. Don't beat yourself up about it, old chap! It's all part of the circle of life.

You see, as time flies because you're having so much fun, there seems to be a sort of decline in the function of certain areas of the brain. The areas of the brain that are involved in short-term memory and problem-solving skills seem to be more affected than others (Wolk & Dickerson, 2020). You might find it easy to remember your son's unapproachable wife or your own husband's family simply because these memories are etched into your brain. This means you do not need to use a large portion of your brain to retrieve them. Newer information, however, like your unapproachable daughter-in-law's latest hairstyle or the color of the newly painted walls may be more difficult to recall because the parts of your brain that remember these new details are somewhat delayed. It's either that, or you just don't care about her hairstyle or the walls. Either way, humor is a great way to help stimulate and sharpen those parts of the brain.

In addition to laughter being great for your brain, it's as contagious as the bubonic plague and may do wonders for building a sense of community among your peers. We are social beings, after all, no matter our age. Even a grumpy old man needs friendship sometimes.

Studies show the actual amount of time spent laughing actually decreases as you age (Greengross, 2013). Well, I say no more! It's time to laugh it up!

So put those varicose veins in your feet up, relax, and get ready to laugh your tooshie off!

With mirth and laughter let old wrinkles come — William Shakespeare, The Merchant of Venice

Part 1: One-Liners

"A day without laughter is a day wasted" – Charlie Chaplin

As you grow older, it's not that your memory is failing you. Oh no. Your memories are all in there, floating around and having a good time. What's failing you is the part in your brain that allows you to access your memories and store new ones.

Since your short-term memory may make it difficult to enjoy a movie, because you just can't remember why Liam Neeson's daughter was "Taken" in the first place, there are still many many things that you can enjoy. Art, for example, is always there, all at once (Blakemore, 2006). There is no beginning that you need to remember or little facts that make the plot more understandable. If you ask me, humor is a form of art!

These one-liners are short, sweet, and overall hilarious!

1. At the talent show last week, in the middle of my boy's performance he fell through the floorboards. He was going through a stage.
2. Why can't you explain puns to a kleptomaniac? Because they always take things literally.
3. I'm afraid for the calendar. Its days are numbered.
4. Why does your dad take an extra pair of socks when he goes golfing? In case he gets a hole in one!
5. Why doesn't the moon need to go to the barber? Because eclipse his hair himself.

6. Where did the boat go when he got sea sick? The dock.

7. After a full day of riding, the bicycle couldn't stand up by itself anymore. It was two-tired.

8. What time did the man go to the dentist? Tooth hurt-y.

9. What's it called when a snowman throws a tantrum? A meltdown.

10.   A guy walks into a bar... and he was disqualified from the limbo contest.

11.   I used to think that facial hair made men look unapproachable... until it grew on me.

12.   How much does Santa pay for parking? Nothing. Parking is on the house.

13.   And the Lord said unto John, "Come forth and you will

receive eternal life." But John came fifth and won a toaster.

14.   My grandfather has the heart of a lion. And that's how he got banned from the zoo.

15.   Why do cows wear bells? Because their horns don't work.

16.   I dated a tennis player once. Love meant nothing to her.

17.   My wife told me to stop impersonating a flamingo. I had to put my foot down.

18.   What did the ocean say to the sand? Nothing. It just waved.

19.   Why are teddy bears never hungry? Because they're stuffed.

20.   Why couldn't the pony sing? He was a little hoarse.

21.   I don't trust lawyers. They're always wearing those fancy lawsuits.

22.   Did you hear about the semicolon that broke the law? He was given two consecutive sentences.

23.   You know how I know I have a clean conscience? I haven't used it a day in my life.

24.   I went to jail once. The police officer said papers and I said scissors. I guess he didn't know the rules.

25.   My wife found out I replaced our bed with a trampoline. She hit the roof.

26.   We just found out that color-blindness runs in the family. The news came out of the purple.

27.   How do you make holy water? You boil the hell out of it.

28.   It's sad that a family can be torn apart by something as simple as a pack of wild dogs.
29.   If life gives you melons, you might be dyslexic.
30.   Letting go of a loved one is hard. But sometimes when you're rock climbing, it's survival of the fittest.

Riddle Me That!

The brain is like a muscle. When it is in use we feel very good. Understanding is joyous. - Carl Sagan

Now, remember when I told you this book is going to challenge your mind and stimulate parts of your brain? Well, welcome to the end of Part 1. You've no doubt read all those one-liners and chuckled or giggled as you saw fit. It is now time to get that old noggin working. It's quite easy to cheat if you'd like. The answer to each question can be found at the end of the book under the section labeled "Why Hello There, Cheater."

"Biology gives you a brain. Life turns it into the mind" – Jefferey Eugenides

Riddle 1

Two friends of mine partook in a competition in which they both had to hold something for as long as possible. The one friend has neither arms or legs and yet he manages to win the competition. What did my two friends hold?

Hint: The answer to this riddle resides in the title of a popular song by the group Berlin written in 1986 for the movie Top Gun (Simpson, 2020). Take your time and try your best! Tom Cruise is quite the hunk in that film, if you ask me. His character left me in awe and inspired my inner fighter pilot. One might even say he took my breath away.

Let's try another.

Riddle 2

It runs as fast as trains and cars but has no legs at all.

It doesn't say a single word although it's mouth's not small.

Through day and night it stays in bed and yet it never sleeps.

It has a head quite high up there and yet it never weeps.

Hint: The answer can be found in the title of a Billy Joel classic that was released in 1993 (Songfacts, 2016). I do believe that in the middle of the night he went walking in his sleep. Justin Timberlake also kindly requested that his former lover cry him this in the hit song that was released in 2002 (Dazed, 2017).

You're on a roll! Okay, one more!

Riddle 3

If you smile at me,

I will smile right back.

If you drop me or crack me,

It's luck you will lack.

What am I?

Hint: The answer to the riddle can be found in Michael Jackson's classic hit that was released in 1987 (Michael Jackson Official Site, 2012). He wanted to make a change for once in his life. It was going to feel really good, going to make a difference, going to make it right. I forget, who was he going to start with again?

Bloody brilliant! I think you've earned the right to move on to Part 2! Let's get going then! You're not getting any younger!

Part 2: Short Stories

Laughter is the sun that drives winter from the human face -Victor Hugo

31. Bury what is dead

In a little complex on the bank of a river there lived a man named George. His house was right on the river's edge, and if you stood in his yard you could hop into the river like the grass was a sort of diving board. One day, some researchers from a local university knocked on George's door and asked if they could have a moment of his time. Being a kind and courteous man, George ushered them in and made a pot of tea. The first to talk was a young man with a ridiculous accent that seemed posher than the queen herself.

"Sir, we have taken samples of the river water from near your complex, and there seems to be many substances in the water that could cause you serious harm. It seems that one of the nearby factories must be dumping chemicals that are found in batteries into the water and causing the fish and plants to die. The pollutants seem to be concentrated right against your yard. We suggest you relocate until we can sort the issue out."

"Those fools," George replied, "I do the decent thing and bury my batteries in the yard when they die."

32. The chatty parrot

There was once a young man who had trouble with the ladies. He was looking for something to make him stand out in a crowd so that he could attract the attention of someone, anyone at all. One day at a flea market, he saw an old lady selling parlor tricks and palm readings. These did not interest him, but her beautiful parrot caught his eye. The lady assured the young man that this parrot was a remarkable one.

"He repeats everything he hears, dear boy," The lady assured him. And so, he bought the parrot and took it home to train it.

The man spoke to the parrot for almost two hours, and when it did not speak back, he grew angry that the lady had lied. So, he went back to the market but found that the lady was no longer there.

He took the parrot to a local veterinarian to test its vocal cords and explained he was assured that the parrot repeats everything it hears.

"It does repeat everything it hears," replied the vet with a smile. "The parrot's vocal cords are perfect but the problem is its deaf."

33. Cracking an egg

There was once a curious boy who never stopped asking grown-ups questions. He would ask about the sky and the stars. The earth and the water. Why wasn't he allowed to drink wine? Why couldn't he drink coffee? Why were his legs so short? Why were his eyes not the same color as his parents'? Then one day, the boy's father was in a bit of a mood and did not have the patience for these questions.

"My son, you ask these questions incessantly and yet you never answer any questions yourself." His father said. "If you can answer only one question for me, then I shall never squeal to answer any of yours ever again. But if you cannot answer my question, then you must promise never to ask me a question again. You must save them for your mother and your grandparents. Do you agree?"

The boy was intrigued. With all the questions he had asked and all the answers he had received, he felt confident that he possessed the knowledge to answer his father's question. So, he agreed.

"Very well," His father began. "How do you throw an egg on the floor without cracking it?" his father asked, giving the boy until the end of the week to come up with an answer.

The boy spent every second of each day thinking about this question. He stole eggs from the refrigerator and spent a whole afternoon gently throwing them. Alas, every egg broke.

By the end of the week, the boy had accepted defeat and made his way to his father's study, holding an egg in his hand.

"I do not know how to throw an egg on the floor without cracking it," the boy looked down as he spoke.

"Bring me the egg and I will show you," His father replied. With that, the boy's father threw the egg at the floor so forcefully that the insides had splattered all over the nearby furniture. The boy was confused and anger built up inside him.

"The egg cracked!" the boy exclaimed, feeling betrayed because he himself had accomplished the same.

"Yes," his father replied with a smile, "but the floor did not. It would be extremely difficult to throw an egg on the floor and crack it."

34.   A husband under stress

A pregnant woman's water broke in the middle of a summer's day while she and her husband were sipping iced tea in the backyard. The woman's contractions had become unbearable within a couple of minutes and she told her husband to bring the car around and call the doctor, informing him they were on their way to the hospital.

When the husband called the hospital, the doctor was not available as he was in the middle of another delivery, so the nurse took the call and tried to calm the man down. He was freaking out, talking incessantly and barely listening to what the nurse was saying.

By the time his wife reached the car, and motioned for her husband to start driving, the nurse had asked how far apart and intense the contractions were.

"Um... my wife says that they're like an eight out of 10 and they're about one minute apart." He told the nurse.

"Alright," the nurse replied. "Is this her first child?"

"No, weren't you listening. This is her husband!"

35. Tip-Toe in the Bathroom

An old man noticed that his wife would always be very quiet in the bathroom. Usually, she would be loud and constantly scream at him for no apparent reason. When she was in the bathroom, however, she was almost silent, tip-toeing and causing little disturbance in the peace. One day he decided to ask his wife's best friend why she was so quiet in the bathroom, so that he may find a way to make her quieter in other parts of the house as well. When he finally understood the reason, he laughed to himself and went along with his day.

Later that evening, he was sitting in the living room, watching his sports channel when his wife came home from her knitting classes. She immediately began her routine of shouting at her husband about his feet on the coffee table and his socks on the floor. When her husband stood up, placed his finger to his lips, pointed at a pill bottle on the table and whispered, "You don't want to wake the sleeping pills, do you?"

36. The Pick-Up Line for Champions

A young man had been searching for love for as long as he could remember. He had tried online dating, speed dating and blind dates. He even tried talking to women he met in public places. Alas, he found no luck.

He had begun to lose hope when he met a woman in a bar one day who began telling him a similar story to his own. She had spent as long as she could remember searching for love and her perfect match. She said she believed her perfect match was out there somewhere, and she would know who he was by a pick-up line that he would use to try to woo her.

The young man felt his heart race as he prepared himself to use a pick-up line to woo the magnificent woman in front of him. At the last moment, he panicked and instead he said, "You've wasted all this time looking for a perfect match when you could have just used a lighter."

37.   The Psychic

A skeptical man accompanied his friend to a psychic one day. He did not believe in anything he did not understand, only what he could see and touch. As his friend finished his session, the psychic turned to the man and asked if he would like a reading. The man, being as skeptical as he was, said he did not believe in magic or spirits and there was nothing the psychic could tell him that would surprise him in any way.

"I understand your beliefs," the psychic said to the man. "But there have also been many like you who have grown to believe once they have experienced a reading. I have not met you before nor do I know anything of your life, but my spirit guide can tell me things that may surprise you."

The man, although still skeptical, decided to humor the psychic and pay for a reading. He sat across from the psychic and offered her his palm. The psychic held his hand and looked in, smiling as she did.

"You are one of two brothers," the psychic started.

Surprised that the lady could know such a thing from simply looking at his palm, the man allowed her to continue.

"Your mother was a teacher and she died from a heart attack," she continued. Once again, the psychic was correct and the man had started to believe.

"You have been married for 10 happy years, and you have two children."

The man got up and smiled triumphantly.

"I knew it!" he said. "This is all some sort of scam! I have three children."

The psychic replied calmly, "That's what you think. Doesn't your youngest look somewhat like your friend Charles?"

38.   The man who knew everyone

There was once a man named David, who claimed to know almost everyone from famous people to convicts. One of his closest friends, who did not believe a single story the man had told, had grown tired of the man's incessant reminders of where he had been and who he had been there with, and so he decided to call the man out on his bluff.

"I bet you don't know Tom Cruise," David's friend said to him one night.

"Tom and I go way back," David replied. "Let's go to Hollywood this weekend. I can introduce you two."

And so, the two men spent the weekend in Hollywood where they met Tom Cruise, who was pleasantly surprised to see his old friend David.

David's friend was not convinced, and so he tried to call his friend out on his bluff once again.

"What about Barack Obama? I bet you don't know him," the friend said to David, to which he calmly replied, "I was there when Michelle and Barack had their first child. They said I'm always welcome in their home. Let's fly to Washington D.C. and you can meet them."

So, the two of them flew to D.C. where they had a pleasant dinner at the Obama's house, but David's friend was not convinced.

"What about the pope?" David's friend asked, finally feeling like he had the upper hand. David could not have known the pope!

"Let's fly to Rome," David said. "I will show you that the pope and I are very familiar."

David and his friend flew to Rome to meet the pope but there were too many people around and David was sure that the pope, with his bad eyesight, would never be able to spot him in the crowd.

"Wait here," David said to his friend. "I know the guards, so they will allow me to enter into the pope's chambers. I will walk out onto the balcony with the pope. Then you must admit that I truly do know everyone," David said triumphantly and then disappeared out of sight.

Keeping to his word, David walked onto the balcony with the pope, waving at the people below. He noticed a crowd gathering in the area where his friend was standing earlier. He ran back down into the courtyard to find that his friend had fainted and a group of people were trying to get him back on his feet.

"What is the matter?" David asked his friend, with concern in his voice.

"Well," his friend replied, "I believe you really do know everyone."

"Didn't I tell you? But why did you faint?"

"When you came out on the balcony with the pope, the man next to me asked out loud, 'Who's that guy up there with David?'" (UpJoke, 2016).

39.   The Clever Little Girl

One day while her mother was chopping up onions, a little girl sat and watched.

"Why are you crying mother?" the little girl asked at the sight of her tears.

"Well, my darling, did you know the only vegetable that can make you cry are onions?" her mother replied.

"Are you sure that they're the only vegetable that can make you cry?" the little girl asked. "Because I bet potatoes could make someone cry as well."

"No, my love," her mother replied. "Only onions can make one cry."

The little clever girl thought about this for a long time and then hurried along to get a potato from the pantry. She ran upstairs to her little brother's room and threw the potato at him, hitting him in the stomach. When her brother began to cry, their mother ran upstairs to see what the commotion was all about.

"You see, mother," the little girl said. "Potatoes can make people cry too."

40.   Human Evolution

One day a curious little boy asked his mother about how humans came to exist. His mother replied, "Well son, one day God made Adam and Eve and they had children who had children who had children, and eventually the entire human population was created."

Being curious and wanting to make sure he understood correctly, he went to his father and asked the same question, to which his father replied, "Well, my boy, a long time ago, apes actually ruled this land, and they evolved into humans. We were once apes, you know?"

Now, more confused than ever, he went back to his mother, and explained what his father had told him.

"Don't be confused, my love," his mother said. "Your father was telling you about his side of the family and I was telling you about mine."

Riddle me that!

The mind is like tofu. It tastes like whatever you marinate it in, - Sylvia Boorstein

I hope you've enjoyed this part of the book, but it's time to challenge that brain of yours again. You know the drill! The answers to the riddles can be found in the section titled "Why hello there, cheater" and I've given you some hints in case you're struggling a little.

Riddle 1

I can't stand the wind
It is ghastly and cold
My life is quite short
I don't live to be old
When alive, I bring light

In the darkest of hours
My life is much shorter
When shaped like a tower

Hint: According to the fabulous and flamboyant Sir Elton John, Princess Diana lived her life much like one of these in the wind, never fading when the sun set or when the rain set in.

Riddle 2

It cannot be seen whenever it's there

It fills up the rooms and spaces like air

Sometimes it's cold but it can be warm

And though it is scary it seldom means harm

It's in the closed closet around all that can fit in

It's found deep inside those who hate kittens

It's always defeated in all those old tales

And is sometimes the form of an evil with scales

Hint: Simon and Garfunkel greeted this as their old friend. They went to talk with it again, you know, when no one dared disturb the sound of silence.

Riddle 3

I'm always by your side, but you see me when there's light
If you're walking by yourself, I may give you quite a fright
Sometimes I am tall, at other times I shrink

Me and you have lots in common, we are closer than you think.

Hint: In the hit Queen song released in 1992, too much love will kill you. Freddie Mercury says, "I'm just the (riddle) of the man I used to be. Too many bitter tears are raining down on me."

Part 3: Oh yes, they actually said that!

I intend to live forever. So far, so good. -Steven Wright

Here are a few funny things that people in real life have actually said.

41. I'm not superstitious, but I am a little stitious. – Michael Scott, The Office

42. I lie to myself all the time. But I never believe me. – S.E. Hinton

43. Love: A temporary insanity curable by marriage. – Ambrose Bierce

44. Before you criticize someone, you should walk a mile in their shoes. That way when you criticize them, you're a mile away from them and you have their shoes. – Jack Handey

45. I have long been of the opinion that if work were such a splendid thing, the rich would have kept more of it for themselves. – Bruce Grocott

46. Truth hurts. Maybe not as much as jumping on a bicycle with the seat missing, but it hurts. – Lt. Frank Drebin, Naked Gun 2 ½: The Smell of Fear

47. I'd like to live like a poor man – only with lots of money. – Pablo Picasso

48. Sometimes I get the feeling that the whole world is against me, but deep down I know that's not true. Some of the smaller countries are neutral. – Robert Orben

49. Be careful of taking health books too seriously. You might die of a misprint. – Mark Twain

50. Laugh, and the whole world laughs with you. Snore and you sleep alone. – Anthony Burgess

51. Suppose you were an idiot. And suppose you were a member of Congress. But I repeat myself. – Mark Twain

52. Life does not cease to be funny when people die any more than it ceases to be serious when people laugh. – George Bernard Shaw

53. I know God promises not to give me more than I can handle. I just wish he didn't trust me so much. – Mother Teresa

54. There's nothing simpler than avoiding people you don't like. Avoiding one's friends, that's the real test. – Dowager Countess Violet Crawley, Downton Abbey

55. If I'm not back in five minutes, just wait longer. – Ace Ventura, Ace Ventura: Pet Detective

56. I really don't think I need buns of steel. I would be happy with buns of cinnamon. – Ellen DeGeneres

57. The man who says that his wife can't take a joke forgets that she took him. – Oscar Wilde

58. We are all on this earth to help others; what the others are here for, I do not know. – W. H. Auden

59. A day without sunshine is like, you know, night. – Steve Martin

60. The secret to staying young is to live honestly, eat slowly and lie about your age. – Lucille Ball

Riddle me that!

Your mind will serve you better than any trinket under the sun...It is a weapon...and like any weapon, you need practice to be any good at wielding it. - Jay Kristoff

It's the end of Part 3, which means a couple more riddles to work that brain of yours. These are a tad more intense and complex than the previous ones. Take your time, and remember, the answers can be found in the section titled "Well hello there, cheater."

Riddle 1

A coat that's best to put on when it is completely wet.

Put the coat on anytime, and simply just forget.

Hint: This one's a bit tricky. The color red is included in addition to the answer to the riddle in a phrase that means to go out and enjoy yourself flamboyantly.

Riddle 2

I'm rooted in the ground below
My roots run strong and deep
Up and up to giant heights
I do become quite steep
The trees look like some little sticks
Compared to my large forms
It took me years to get this way
I'm closest to the storms

Hint: A popular pop/soul song sung by Marvin Gaye in 1967 claims that there are none high enough to keep him from getting to his baby. There also "ain't no valley low enough" and "ain't no river wide enough."

Riddle 3

When you need me, you throw me out,
When you don't need me, you pull me back.

Hint: Although the answer to the riddle refers to an object, the same word can be used to refer to something or someone that gives support or even the member of a team that goes last in a relay (Cambridge Dictionary, 2019).

Bonus riddle because I've grown quite fond of you!

I am with you day and night,
Every moment, not in sight
When I break, it makes you sad
I can thump when you are mad

You can hear me in your head
When I stop, then you are dead.

Hint: Elton John asked Kiki Dee not to go breaking this of his, to which she replied she couldn't if she tried.

Part 4: Family issues

Happiness is having a large loving, caring, close-knit family... in another city. - George Burns

Let's call this number **61** since my life is a joke.

I thought I'd use this exercise as a bit of a catharsis. I can rant about my family while you can laugh about my misfortunes. Fun! Fun! Fun!

Family is as hard as rocks that are being thrown at you repeatedly for no apparent reason. I know, because a couple of my family members just recently moved in with me after financial difficulties on all their parts. If you ask me, it sounds like poor investments and lack of self-control. I've tried to find families as dysfunctional as mine in the past to compare notes, of course, but one seems not to exist. Before they all moved in, I used to have a handle on life, but I'm pretty sure one of them broke it and is trying to play it cool. Much like my state-of-the-art mosaic vase from Tuscany.

My mother used to tell me that there is no such thing as a perfect family. That all families have their problems and there are probably some people out there who have a worse family life than we do. Let me tell you, you can't spell *families* without *lies*.

Right after my family moved in, my girlfriend left me. It didn't bother me that much because I planned to break up with her at the end of that week anyway. It's not that I have anything against vegetarians, I just don't think that my ancestors fought their way to the top of the food chain to share a diet with rabbits and goats, that's all.

My mother is simply an awful person. She's rude and obnoxious and I'm pretty sure her presence in the neighborhood is the reason more than five houses on our street have "for sale" signs outside. She made me remove the welcome mat from outside the front door because she said she refuses to be a liar. I swear, her bottom is probably jealous of all that crap that comes out her mouth. I wonder how my father, God rest his soul, dealt with her for all those years.

My mother and father had a special relationship, that's for sure. When he was about 80 years old, the doctor told them both that if his heart rate increases any more, he's definitely going to have a heart attack and die. The next day, my mother told him that she was pregnant. Turned out to be a false alarm, but my father didn't make it to hear the news. To be honest, my mother and father were both happy for about 25 years, and then they met. I learned a lot from their marriage. One thing I learned is that every married person should forget their mistakes. There's really no point in two people remembering the same thing.

My father was a drunk. He drank so much that one birthday he blew out the candles and almost burned the place down. I remember it so clearly. My mother was holding the cake and when my father blew, her wig caught on fire. Then he passed out on the floor, which my mother saw as an opportunity to sell his car, which he loved more than us, for just enough money to buy a new wig, some milk, and a packet of jelly beans.

Now, I was raised as an only child, which drove my sister insane. She was one of those troubled youths but she always had a lot of love to give. That's why by 17, she had her first kid and now I lose count of how many of those demons are running around. I do believe that a couple years ago she got one of those giant teddy bears for the middle kid. She was really into stuffed animals and to this day she says it was one of the best trades she had ever made. I think the kid ended up living with a rich family in the south, so really, he's the one that got away. When I saw her the day before she moved in, she had the biggest diamond ring I had ever seen. When I asked to see it, she told me that it came with a curse. Naturally, I forbade her from bringing that thing any closer to me, and demanded that she get rid of it immediately. Then she explained that the curse was her new husband and that he was moving in too.

My sister's youngest kid is cute as can be, but as dumb as a doorknob, I tell you. He hit me with a can of soda the other day and when I told him that it hurt, he said that didn't make sense because his daddy told him it was a soft drink. Kids.

For what it's worth, my new brother-in-law doesn't seem like a bad guy at all. The other day I overheard him trying to teach one of the kids some kind of life lesson. "When life gives you lemons," he was saying, "you make lemonade that's strong and pungent.

Then you throw that sour juice into the eyes of the fool who gave you those lemons and demand for the oranges that you had initially asked for!" What can I say? The standards were set pretty low after my sister's first couple boyfriends.

I remember she once dated this guy who worked in the traffic department at the local municipality. There was a rumour going around that he was stealing on the job, which my sister insisted was a lie. Then one day, I visited him at his place for some reason and all the signs were there. I'm a little ashamed to say that I stole a stop sign and put it outside our childhood home so that there were always witnesses and my mother couldn't spank us in the yard anymore.

Here's to hoping the ninth time's the charm!

I have observed that my sister and brother-in-law do seem to fight quite a lot. Just the other day I heard them arguing about switching their daughter's weekly English tuition for martial arts classes. My brother-in-law insisted that actions speak louder than words. Bless his soul.

My other nephew thinks he's hilarious, but he refuses to tell jokes around glass. He's scared it could crack up. He's not the brightest bulb in the pack, I can tell you that. He definitely didn't get any of my genes. One night he swallowed a coin just for the fun of it, and as he felt it dropping into his stomach he began to cry. He was convinced that he was going to die then and there, even though my sister tried to explain that he's likely to find the coin in the toilet the next morning. He would hear nothing at all until his father placed a similar coin in the palm of his hand and then placed his palm against the boy's tummy, pretending that he drew it out from the inside. In surprise and exhilaration, the daft boy grabbed the coin, swallowed it and said, "Do it again, daddy!" He's 16 years old. There's nothing you can do about bad genes. The kid's not bad looking, though, maybe he can make it in the modeling business. You know what they say, the speed of light travels faster than the speed of sound. That's why people look sharp before they open their mouths.

Now, the little one, he has a face like a saint. A Saint Bernard that is. He's going to grow up to be an ugly man.

One time I was trying to explain the concept of death to him and he was insisting that all parts of the body die at different times. Apparently the pupils dilate.

I'm proud of the 16-year-old, though. When he was 12, he got himself addicted to the hokey pokey... and then he mustered up the courage to turn himself around.

My brother, who moved in before the rest of them, lost his job earlier on. He used to be a manager at one of those juice factories, but he got fired because he couldn't really concentrate. He brought home samples one day. I swear to God it tasted like water to me.

His wife used to work at the calendar factory, but then they fired her for no apparent reason. I remember her crying that day and yelling, "All I did was take a day off." She's not that great of a cook either, and she's gotten a little chunky since the last time I saw her. I have to tell you, she burned 2,000 calories the other day. I told her not to leave the brownies in the oven for that long, but who listens to me?

One of my cousins is a kleptomaniac. When it gets really bad, she just takes something. And not small things like pens or pencils. Oh no. She took the TV last week and sold it for money to pay for these pills, which I assume are working because I just can't seem to get her to take those things.

There's another cousin that lives with us on most days, but I haven't seen him in a couple of weeks. He was going for some sort of job interview that required an impromptu drug test. The test came back negative so he got the job, but that afternoon he went out looking for his dealer to ask him a couple questions. I'm sure he'll be back soon enough.

I have another cousin on my father's side who's not all there either. He's being sued by an airline after working for them for almost a decade. Apparently, after having a big argument with his teenage daughter about a boy she was dating, he lost it at work. He worked as a flight attendant you see, and when it was time to explain how to use the oxygen face masks in case of emergency, his rehearsed speech went somewhat out the window and was replaced with, "In the event of an emergency oxygen masks will descend from the ceiling. Please fasten your mask before those of your child or other dependant. If you have more than one child, I guess we'll find out who your favorite is." Then he looked at the passenger closest to him and said, "I suggest fastening your boy's mask on first. Get rid of the girl before she grows to those unbearable teenage years," So, he's unemployed if you know anyone who's hiring.

There used to be a great aunt who lived with us as well. Every Thursday is game night, you see, and my mother insists that everyone be involved. My great aunt loved game night. Although, I must say, the worst possible time to have a heart attack is during a game of charades. You see, because of the different levels of players in the game, we don't play with a timer. So, it took us almost an hour to realize she wasn't breathing. It was only when my nephew guessed "Death at a Funeral" that we began to panic. I was pretty calm, if you ask me. Later, my mother mentioned that if anyone can remain in a state of calm when everyone around them is panicking, that person clearly does not appreciate the severity of the situation. And that's the thanks I get for housing the old lady under my very own roof.

The worst part about the entire family living with me is the doctor's appointments. My mother had neck pain so she forced me to take her to our family physician. I had asked my cousin the kleptomaniac, but she said she was busier than a one-legged man in a kicking contest. She was probably just planning her next big heist. If you ask me, my mother's neck pain is probably from the inability to hold her big head up every second of every day. Anyways, while I was there the doctor told me that obesity runs in my family. I'm pretty sure nobody runs in my family and I don't remember a cousin named "obesity" but he'd know better than me. He's been our family physician for a long time now.

The point is, if you're sitting out there thinking that your family is difficult to deal with, then you better go and give that good-for-nothing son of yours a big fat hug and tell him how much you love him!

Now that you've read about my less than ideal family and you're feeling very grateful for your very own, let's get that brain working again, shall we?

Riddle me that!

Riddle 1

I have many keys but they do not open locks.
I have legs as well, but I cannot wear socks.

Hint: Billy Joel released a song in 1973 about it, of which the name contains the answer to the riddle (Smooth Radio, 2018). I do believe it began at about 9 o'clock on a Saturday. The regular crowd shuffles in. There was an old man sitting next to him, making love to his tonic and gin.

Riddle 2

You see me in the air
But I am not a kite
I am what you see
When water refracts light

Hint: A song with the answer to the riddle in the title was sung in 1938 by Judy Garland for the movie *The Wizard of Oz (Songwriters Hall of Fame, 2014)*.

Riddle 3

Never was,

I am always to be.
No one ever saw me,
nor ever will.
And yet I am the confidence of all,
to live and breathe on this terrestrial ball.
What am I?

Hint: In Doris Day's famous song, *Que Sera Sera,* when she asked her mother if she would be pretty or rich, her mother simply replied Que Sera Sera, whatever will be will be. The (*answer to the riddle*) is not ours to see. Que Sera Sera.

Part 5: Old is funny too!

The important thing to remember is that I'm probably going to forget. - Anonymous

62. How times have changed. My grandma just stopped to help a teenager glued to her phone cross the street safely.

63. What do my grandmother and a bee have in common? They both hum because they can never remember the lyrics.

64. I went to live with my grandparents one summer so that I could take care of them. I never knew how much they needed me until a local politician was taking donations toward building a swimming pool and my

grandparents took a bucket of water to the rally.

65. Today my grandfather told me that if he ever died after choking on gummy bears, I should tell his old army buddies that he was killed by bears.

66. My grandma broke her hip in two places. When I called the doctor to tell him to be expecting us, he told me to tell her not to go to those two places anymore.

67. My grandfather went to the doctor about his memory problems and the first thing they made him do was pay.

68. My grandfather told the doctor that he gets heartburn every time he eats a birthday cake. The doctor told him to take off the candles next time.

69. My grandfather's best friend was tired of the steep medical bills from the doctor. He was the only doctor in town and had just about had enough of the guy. He couldn't understand why the prescriptions were so hard to read and the bills were so damn clear. Then he got an idea. There was a police officer who lived on his street, so one night, he graffitied the police officer's house. He made the writing look so difficult to read that the court was convinced it was the doctor.

70. Once, my mother visited the doctor to get one of those routine check-ups. It wasn't meant to be anything serious, but then the doctor told her that she was seriously ill.

"I'm very sorry," he said, "but you're seriously ill. Is there anyone you'd like me to call for you?

"Yes," my mother replied, "Another doctor."

And I kid you not, she lived another 50 years after that.

71. Advice from my grandmother

My grandmother gives better advice than Dr Phil!

- Alcohol is a great solvent. It dissolves marriages, families and careers.
- When a baby is born, do not be alarmed. You need to calm yourself down and just borrow some money.
- Always go swimming with a friend. That way, the chances of you getting eaten by a shark go down by 50%.
- Everyone thinks their baby is the smartest and cutest and most

well behaved. Well, you're wrong! Your kid is probably stupid and ugly but you just can't see it. And I'm pretty sure he bit the dog the other day. If you're going to be a parent, you need to start being realistic.

- If you're the one they hand the camera to when someone says "let's take a group photo," then you're the ugly one in the group.

- Don't call me old. I'm only going to be old in 15 years' time.

- If you ever mistakenly fart in public, just scream "Jet Power!" and start to walk faster.

- If you ever kill someone and they deserve it, bury the body and then plant a garden of endangered plants over it. It's illegal to dig up endangered plants.

- I can tell you and the hubby aren't seeing eye to eye. Let me tell you, the best way to get him to do something is to suggest that maybe he's too old to do it.
- Time may heal all my wounds, but it's a lousy beautician.
- If you let aging get you down, soon your joints will be all stiff and you'll struggle to get back up.
- Don't drink downstream from a cow herd. Just go inside and drink from the tap.
- Save all your old tea bags that don't have any juice left in them. If you're having a bad day at work, just put one of those old teabags in a glass of whiskey. That way your colleagues won't judge you. Don't forget to blow on the whiskey now and again to convince everyone that it's tea.

- In life you need focus and concentration. That's why you should never break more than one law at a time. That's how you'll get caught.

- Lean in and whisper to your kids when they do something wrong. It's scarier than yelling.

- Start all your phone conversations with "My phone is almost dead, but we can still talk." That way, you can hang up any time.

- If you can help it, only date orphans. That way you don't have to worry about in-laws.

- If you want people to listen to what you have to say, claim that it's something that your father told you.

- Health just means that you're dying at a slower rate than me. But you're still dying so sit down.
- Get into the habit of not introducing yourself to others. Let someone else introduce you. Because when you get to my age, it might just be an old friend you forgot about.
- The way I attract the men is instead of calling my bathroom "The John," I call it "The Jim." That way I'm not really lying when I say I go to the Jim first thing in the morning and spend most of my time there.
- You should marry a man your age or older. That way your beauty will fade at a similar rate to his eyesight.
- If you ever watch one of those videos where someone says,

"Don't try this at home," then try it at your friend's house.

- If you ever rub a lamp and a genie appears but he tells you that you can't wish for more wishes... wish for more genies.
- If you ever get caught sleeping on the job, try to keep your cool. Raise your head slowly and say "In Jesus name, Amen."
- Don't count your chickens before they hatch, because those might be snake eggs.

72. The perfect marriage

There was a man and a woman who were married to each other for almost their whole lives. They had a very honest and open relationship; they kept no secrets from each other, except for a little box that the old lady kept in the corner of her cupboard that she asked her husband never to ask about. The old man loved his wife dearly and never asked about the box or its contents.

One day, the old lady had grown very ill and the doctors seemed very concerned about her condition. The doctor advised the old man that he should sort out her affairs as best as he could, because his wife may not see the end of the week. After discussing everything with his wife, the old man asked if he may look inside the box and see what it contained. The old lady agreed, telling her husband to bring the box to the hospital so they could open it together.

The old man brought the box to the hospital, as promised, and opened it in front of his wife to find that it contained three crocheted dolls and the biggest stack of money he had ever seen. He looked at his wife for an explanation, and so she began.

"When we married, my mother told me that the secret to a great marriage is to never argue. Instead, she said that every time you made me mad, I should crochet a doll quietly and allow my anger to subside."

The man looked at the three dolls and tears filled his eyes. That meant that there were only three occasions that his love had felt anger towards him in their many years of marriage.

"My love," the man replied. "And what about the money?"

"Oh," his wife replied. "That's the money I made from selling the dolls."

73. When memory fails you

There was an elderly billionaire who had just married a woman 40 years younger than him. He was in his 60s, the woman was in her 20s, and they lived happily together. One day, the billionaire, being quite famous in the area, was seen sitting on a park bench at the local park and crying. Another man around the same age as him, sat beside him and started to comfort him.

"What is wrong?" the man asked the billionaire.

"I have a wife at home who is the epitome of beauty and grace. She cooks like an angel and every night we share a bottle of wine while feasting on all my favorite food. She is caring and kind. She rubs my back when it hurts and allows me to control the TV. She lets me drink with my friends on Sundays and wears the skimpiest of outfits when we are out together. She is absolutely perfect." The billionaire manages to say through his tears.

"I don't understand," replied the man. "You sound very happy. Why are you crying?"

"I have forgotten where I live, kind sir," the billionaire replied.

Riddle me that!

Now that you've had a good laugh at yourself and those around you (get it, because they're old as well) let's get some of those brain juices flowing again!

Riddle 1

Some say that I heal anything
Although I may leave scars
Some say that I destroy all things
Including all the stars
Some wish that I could just stand still
To savour all good times
And even though I wish I could
You must feel sad sometimes
I am the strongest force of all
All men wish they had more
One day I will run out for you
So get out there! Explore!

Hint: If you were Cindy Lauper's man in 1983, her song that contains the answer to the riddle would be written for you. " If you're lost, you can look and you will find me ..."

Riddle 2

I can be calm but also not
I answer to the moon
There's more to me than meets the eye
I rage during monsoons
I hide the creatures of the deep
I give them homes and care
My beauty is like nothing else
No other things compare

Hint: The answer is also the surname of a recording artist in the 70s and 80s that had Trinidadian heritage. One of his most famous songs is "When the going gets tough." He also sings "Suddenly, life has new meaning to me," and his first name is Billy.

Riddle 3

I possess a halo of water, walls of stone and a tongue of wood. For very long have I stood.

Hint: (okay this is an easy one) Kings and queens would live in these in the days of old. A man's home is also said to be his...?

Part 6: BONUS! Some Dark Comedy

I do believe the quickest way to a man's heart is not through his stomach. It's through his chest, with an axe. - A woman scorned.

This section is a little bonus for all you folks out there with a dark and sinister sense of humor. If you're a particularly sensitive or emotional individual, I suggest you skip this part and go straight on to the conclusion of this book. Don't say I didn't warn you.

74. Did you hear about my buddy Jeff? He just got his left side amputated. He's all right now.

75. What's the most difficult part of a vegetable to eat? The wheelchair.

76. When you see the names of lovers engraved on trees you shouldn't find it cute or romantic. You should be concerned about how many young people are carrying knives with them on dates.

77. My wife and I have recently decided that we don't want children. If anybody else would like them, please contact me and we can arrange a pick-up time.

78. How do you stop a conversation between deaf people? Switch off the lights.

79. I have a step ladder because my real ladder left when I was just a kid.

80. I stole my ex-girlfriend's wheelchair. Guess who came crawling back to me?

81. Why did the mailman die? Because everyone dies eventually.

82. How are friends like snow? If you pee on them, they disappear.

83. My granddaughter's acne is really getting out of hand. Yesterday my blind friend started reading her face.

84. Last time I visited a buddy of mine, he told me to make myself at home. So, I threw him out. I hate visitors.

85. Why can't orphans play baseball? They don't know where home is.

86. Did you know that Germany came up with sparkling water? Who else would think of adding gas to something?

87. How do you punish a blind kid if they do something bad? Rearrange the furniture.

88. My grandfather came back from the war with one leg. He refuses to tell us who's leg it was and why he brought it all this way.

89. There's a rumor going around that I'm a gambler. I don't know who started that rumor but I bet serious money it's that good for nothing Jeffery.

90. When my father told me that I was adopted, he explained that one man's trash is another man's treasure.

91. Where did Sally go when the bomb went off? Everywhere.

92. What do you call a dog with no legs? It doesn't matter what you call him, he won't come anyway.

93. Why don't librarians lend out books about suicide? Because they know they won't get it back.

94. I bought my blind friend a cheese grater for his birthday. About a week later, he called me to say that he couldn't finish the book, it was too violent.

95. So Stephen Hawking walked into a bar... just kidding.

96. Kid: "Dad, can we get ice-cream?"

 Dad: "Hey, until we get the paternity results it's James to you, kid."

97. Why did Princess Diana cross the road? She didn't wear a seatbelt.

98. What's blue and doesn't fit anymore? A dead epileptic.

99. What's worse than finding a worm in your apple? The Holocaust

100. Why do orphans like playing tennis? It's the only love that they get.

And that's 100 jokes to brighten up your day and get the giggle juices flowing.

Why Hello There, Cheater!

Part 1

Riddle 1: Breath

Riddle 2: River

Riddle 3: Mirror

Part 2

Riddle 1: Candle

Riddle 2: Darkness

Riddle 3: Shadow

Part 3

Riddle 1: Paint

Riddle 2: Mountain

Conclusion

Now, although the jokes in this book were meant to brighten your day, the real gems in here are the riddles! You see, in addition to the riddle testing your memory and stimulating the parts of your brain that are important for making decisions, like whether to eat the pasta or the steak for lunch today, the hints are also tied to songs and artists.

Music is one of the best ways to stimulate the portion of your brain responsible for memory as well as emotion (Team, 2018). I'm sure you've experienced feeling happy when a song comes on the radio or feeling nostalgic when you hear your wedding song again. That's because the song is tied to a memory that allows you to feel those emotions. Let's take right now, for example. What song is playing in the background while you're reading this part of the book? Classical? Hip-Hop? Pop? Or maybe no music is playing at all. Do me a favor, will you. Play a song you've heard before and read this paragraph again. I guarantee you, next time you hear the same song in the mall while walking with your friends or in the car on your way to your daughter's house, you'll remember this book and the way it made you feel.

So, next time you want to find a way to remember something, put on some good music and dance to it as you carry on with your day!

And remember,

Youthfulness is about how you live, not when you were born! - Karl Lagerfeld

References

Alzheimer's Society. (2019). Memory tools - using words and rhymes. Alzheimer's Society. https://www.alzheimers.org.uk/get-support/staying-independent/memory-tools-using-words-and-rhymes#content-start

April 16, B. L. E., & 2021. (2021, April 16). 50 Funny Short Jokes That Guarantee a Laugh. Best Life. https://bestlifeonline.com/funny-short-jokes/

Awesome Inventions. (2018, January 9). The Best And Worst Funny Pieces Of Advice From Dads. Awesome Inventions. https://www.awesomeinventions.com/funny-pieces-of-advice-from-dads/

Belz, K. (2021, February 12). 35+ Jokes For Seniors That'll Make Them Laugh No Matter What. Scary Mommy. https://www.scarymommy.com/jokes-seniors/

Blakemore, B. (2006, July). Art Awakens Alzheimer's Patients' Minds. ABC News. https://abcnews.go.com/WNT/Health/Story?id=2146253&page=1

Blumenthal, J. (2011, December 4). 35 Classic One-liners About Aging. HuffPost. https://www.huffpost.com/entry/aging-comedy_b_1128087

Cambridge Dictionary. (2019). anchor. Dictionary.cambridge.org. https://dictionary.cambridge.org/dictionary/english/anchor

Cavoto, E. (2021, June 3). 100 of the Corniest Dad Jokes to Make You Laugh Out Loud. The Pioneer Woman. https://www.thepioneerwoman.com/home-lifestyle/a35617884/best-dad-jokes/

Dazed. (2017, November 24). An ode to Britney: the making of the Cry Me A River video. Dazed. https://www.dazeddigital.com/music/article/38186/1/cry-me-a-river-justin-timberlake-video-director-interview

Greengross, G. (2013). Humor and Aging - A Mini-Review. Gerontology, 59(5), 448–453. https://doi.org/10.1159/000351005

Henderson, S. (2015, March 31). Laughter and Learning: Humor Boosts Retention. Edutopia; George Lucas Educational Foundation. https://www.edutopia.org/blog/laughter-learning-humor-boosts-retention-sarah-henderson

Jacob, S. (2017, March 30). 16 Hilarious Doctor Jokes Because Laughter Really Is The Best Medicine. Www.scoopwhoop.com. https://www.scoopwhoop.com/doctor-jokes/

Khurana, S. (2020). Funny Quotes From Famous People. LiveAbout. https://www.liveabout.com/famous-funny-quotes-2832412

Kuehn, K. (2021, May 6). 50 Long Riddles to Give Your Brain a Workout. Reader's Digest. https://www.rd.com/article/long-riddles/

Liles, M. (2021, May 14). 101 Good, Clean Jokes That'll Make You Laugh Your Pants Off. Parade: Entertainment, Recipes, Health, Life, Holidays. https://parade.com/1041830/marynliles/clean-jokes/

Michael Jackson Official Site. (2012). Man In The Mirror | Michael Jackson Official Site. Michael Jackson Official Site. https://www.michaeljackson.com/track/man-mirror/

Nelson, J. (2018, June 11). 50+ Funny One Liners To Tell Friends. Thought Catalog. https://thoughtcatalog.com/january-nelson/2018/06/funny-one-liners/

Painter, S. (2016). 15 Hilarious (but Clean) Jokes for the Elderly. LoveToKnow. https://seniors.lovetoknow.com/Jokes_for_the_Elderly

Parade. (2021, January 12). 101 Funny Quotes That Will Make You LOL! (And They're All Safe for Work). Parade: Entertainment, Recipes, Health, Life, Holidays. https://parade.com/940913/parade/funny-quotes/

Reader's Digest. (2021). Too Much Time. Reader's Digest. https://www.rd.com/jokes/one-liners/

Simpson, D. (2020, November 16). How we made: Take My Breath Away, the Top Gun theme tune by Berlin. The Guardian. https://www.theguardian.com/music/2020/nov/16/giorgio-moroder-take-my-breath-away-top-gun-how-we-made-berlin-tom-cruise

Smooth Radio. (2018). The Story of... "Piano Man" by Billy Joel. Smooth.

https://www.smoothradio.com/features/billy-joel-piano-man-lyrics-meaning-facts/

SolveOrDie. (2016). 7 riddles about ocean - SOLVE or DIE. Solveordie.com. https://solveordie.com/riddles-about-ocean/

Songfacts. (2016). The River Of Dreams by Billy Joel - Songfacts. Www.songfacts.com. https://www.songfacts.com/facts/billy-joel/the-river-of-dreams

Songwriter's Hall of Fame. (2014). Over the Rainbow | Songwriters Hall of Fame. Songhall.org. https://www.songhall.org/awards/winner/over_the_rainbow

Team Scary Mommy. (2019, October 7). 108 One-Liner Jokes As Punny As They Are Funny. Scary Mommy. https://www.scarymommy.com/one-liner-jokes/

Team, S. (2018). Which Genres Of Music Improve Your Memory. Www.connollymusic.com. https://www.connollymusic.com/stringovation/which-genres-of-music-improve-your-memory#:~:text=Other%20studies%20have%20found%20that

Texas, E. O. of. (2016). Clean Senior Citizen Jokes & Cartoons | Funny Maxine Quotes. Www.elderoptionsoftexas.com. https://www.elderoptionsoftexas.com/jokes.htm

The Grand Theater Blackpool. (2021, March 28). Funniest Ever Jokes And Best One-Liners From The Greatest Comedians. Blackpool Grand Theatre. https://www.blackpoolgrand.co.uk/funniest-ever-jokes-one-liners

UpJoke. (2016). The 99+ Best Skeptic Jokes - ↑UPJOKE↑. Upjoke.com. https://upjoke.com/skeptic-jokes

Upjoke. (2018). The 94+ Best Alzheimer Jokes - ↑UPJOKE↑. Upjoke.com. https://upjoke.com/alzheimer-jokes

Wolk, D. A., & Dickerson, B. C. (2020, December). UpToDate. Www.uptodate.com. https://www.uptodate.com/contents/clinical-features-and-diagnosis-of-alzheimer-disease?source=history_widget

Made in the USA
Monee, IL
06 February 2023

27252147R00059